This is the book you'll want tucked in your satchel at riverside or mountaintop, wherever you find your deepest breaths. What does it mean to inhabit one's life fully—as a mother, as an artist, as a collector of trees, birds, stones, a hundred particular griefs? She chronicles the ruin of every little thing, holds her daughters close, Kristina Moriconi writes in this work of caesura and human song. In her sage lyric narrative, Moriconi looks askance at the antiquated myths girls ingest on their way to womanhood and offers, in their place, truer lessons: Our bodies can break open again and again, we can learn to forgive ourselves, we can carry a heart heavy with the processing and reprocessing of the body's blood, love, and ache. We can love multitudinously. *In the Cloakroom of Proper Musings* is a beautiful and significant work I will be returning to for years.

DARLA HIMELES, Author of *Flesh Enough*

# In the
# Cloakroom
## of Proper Musings

*a lyric narrative*

by Kristina Moriconi

*atmosphere press*

for Samantha and Alison, for teaching me
the meaning of unconditional love

&

for Jeanne, in gratitude for the many hours
spent with me in the Office of Guidance,
for gifting me words like *acceptance* and *forgiveness*,
helping me learn how to use them in a sentence

*She sees her reflection ... She looks at herself and I stare back.*

*She seems to have startled herself. Who are we, now that we have to rely on new ways of calculating the integers of time?*

—Judith Kitchen

In the Magnet School for Unexpected Mothers, she reads about the kind of mother she wants to be.

But there is no adequate warning.

Now, there will always be things in need of reckoning.

That needle needs to be slipped into the smallest space between the bones of her spine. With paper crinkling and tearing beneath her on the table, she needs to bend forward more. And more. Even though her belly is still big and round with baby.

She needs to be on the other side of a drape hung just above her waist, so she will not see her daughter come through the egress they've made of her abdomen.

She needs to know everything is okay. She needs to know how not to be afraid.

But there are bullies here in this Boarding School for New Mothers. They say things that make her cry.

She needs to take her baby home. To build a nest for them in the shadow of moonlight. She needs to let herself be flawed, to fumble through. To sort out cupboards and alphabetize baby books on a shelf. To knit a blanket she'll never finish.

To know the movement of her body is enough.

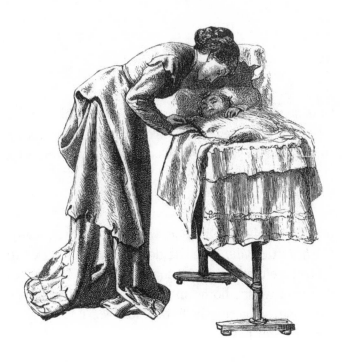

In the Home School for New Mothers, a safer, quieter space, her own mother, *Nana*, shines in a way she has never seen before, shows her how to bathe and swaddle her little one. How to sing *Rock a bye baby on the tree top. When the wind blows the cradle will rock.*

*When the bough breaks, the cradle will fall...*

She makes a mental note to find some other songs to lull her baby to sleep.

This one seems cruel to her now. Reckless.

❧

Outside the nursery window, bees form a hive in the eaves of the house. A giant oak bends and sways, casts shadows of its shifting limbs on the floor beside her.

So much looms.

Inside, as night falls, she whisper-sings a lullaby. *Hush, Little Baby.* But she doesn't like the words to this song either. First, she changes *Papa* to *Mama.* But that isn't what's bothering her. It's the list of things the song suggests she'll buy for her baby girl in exchange for her bedtime silence:

A mockingbird. A diamond ring. A looking glass. A billy goat. A cart and bull. A dog named Rover. A horse and cart.

She hasn't showered in days. Her eyes are puffy and red. She paces the hall with a teething baby perched on her hip. And song lyrics that once seemed soothing to her sound like nothing more than a bribe.

*Although the mockingbird might be nice right now,* she thinks, *with its repertoire of nearly two hundred tunes.*

Her second daughter tries twice to come too soon. The third time, just a week early, she is born.

Days before, a tropical depression brings howling winds, pounding rain. As the storm intensifies, she stands on the front porch of a small house in a small town beside a husband she hardly knows.

Twice, her body has bloomed, made a home for their babies.

Not once has he marveled at the changing shape of her belly.

Not once has he pressed his hands against the jutting bones, wanting to feel the movement, his own blood orbiting.

Her water breaks in that house. One last beginning before an end.

By now, she can barely hold on.

She loses herself somewhere between pushing and trying to pump breastmilk from a body that has declared its own drought.

Fever-sick and hallucinating, she sees saints with stigmata, hears them chant *hallelujah-praise-be*, a chorus of promises to save her.

Time is a tightrope-walk. A knife-juggle.

✠

She is trying to balance a crown on her head.

And a stack of unpaid bills.

And parents with matching hypertension and pack-a-day lungs.

And pages from a perpetually half-finished book.

And a sticky-note-obsessed boss with bad coffee breath.

And a week-old Pop-Tart.

And a less-than-half-interested husband.

And two small pecking birds.

That year, she plants her first vegetable garden in the backyard.

She becomes preoccupied with the invasion of a rabbit family, starts forgetting to water her prized geraniums in the hanging baskets, even after their petals wilt, their leaves shrivel. They all die.

She talks to the neighbors. Brings a pile of gardening books home from the library. Tries chicken wire first. Then granular repellant. Then an ultrasonic motion-activated machine.

Then an organic mixture of water, dish soap, hot sauce, and garlic cloves.

Nothing works.

She gives up. Lets the weeds take over. And the growing fluffle of rabbits.

On her second Halloween, the last one before the marriage ends, the youngest is a dinosaur. It's an easy costume, a lot like pajamas so it won't be difficult to dress or undress her. She can be a bit feisty, especially in the evening if she hasn't taken a nap during the day.

There are overstuffed dinosaur feet that are supposed to slip on over her sneakers, but she doesn't like them.

Her father insists. *What kind of dinosaur doesn't have big green feet?* he asks.

She wants to respond: *A two-year-old tired one.* But she doesn't. Instead, she comforts her daughter who is already crying and starting to stiffen her limbs.

She recognizes this. Phase One, DEFCON 5.

*The costume is ruined,* he says, stomping out of the room. *You give in to her all the time.*

He slams the door as he leaves, as though this kind of punctuation is needed.

Christmas that year is the Year of the Dollhouse. Her husband promises he'll help her put it together, but then he's never home. Or he's too tired.

She follows the instruction booklet, night after night, tools splayed out on the floor around her. More often than not, a string of quiet obscenities spills from her mouth.

Laser-cut unfinished wood, letter-stamped, for *easy* tab-slot assembly. *Bleep. Bleep.*

Small pieces of gingerbread trim. *Bleeping-bleep bleep.* Several layers of skin on her left thumb and index finger lost to Krazy Glue.

In the end, she remains unsure about the structural integrity of the house's second floor.

Thankfully, the dolls are small.

May marks the beginning of moth season. It is the month when she decides to leave him, to devise a plan. Slowly. Methodically. She will need to prepare. Her daughters are two and four years old.

One night, from the front porch, she hears him yell at the two-year-old who is upstairs crying: *Shut the fuck up!*

She hums a song from her childhood, one her own father used to sing. But the words don't come.

Above her head, moths circle the porch light, smack up against the glass globe. She finds one on the floor, its gray mottled wings contracted. Still. She sits beside it, gathers her knees up against her chest, draws her arms tight around them. Makes herself small.

&

Inside the house, there's a chair in the living room that rocks.

Next, she longs to write: *where she cradles her children.*

But she wants to select more honest words. To name the unbearable.

The truth is: she cries there in that corner beside the two-windowed wall. The blinds kept closed day and night, she's forgotten that once-upon-a-time there'd been light.

&

She has never cooked anything in the oven, though it stands there commanding her attention, stark black cast iron against the palest yellow wall.

The room is dark. Dirty dishes stacked in the sink.

And there are tiny voices demanding food.

Her life is a series of inner-conflicts—how to exist, to be, in this world where the only instruction manual warns: *Beware. Combustible.*

&

Sometimes, she sleeps on the floor.

The bed is empty and, if she stares long enough, she sees the shape of him in the Ralph Lauren sheets.

And the lies.

And the nights spent awake, turned toward the wall.

By morning, the small bones of her spine ache.

In the hallway, she still hears the sound of his screams, words children should never hear.

On a Sunday, she leaves with her daughters, doesn't want them to grow up thinking love is a loud, angry voice.

As President of the Home Economics Club,
she wants to show everyone what it means
to make a home.

The first apartment she finds for them is small.

It fills up fast with doubt.

She hangs up curtains that let in some light. On one of the walls, she brightens the room with art projects they bring home to her. Construction paper and glue, crayons and paint, handprints and rainbows and red-glitter hearts.

Still, she worries. Always on edge.

But, when the two of them come bounding out of their new bedroom, giggling, dragging their beanbag chairs behind them, she lets go of her uncertainty, collapses in between their small bodies.

The three of them huddle together, make up stories about mermaids washing ashore, marooned in the middle of their living room, its sail-white walls, its seafoam floor.

At the Public School of Noble and Unselfish Purposes, she nearly fails all of her final exams.

*Too much is unfixable,* she thinks. *Broken dolls and bruises. Socks left unmatched and ones in need of mending.*

She never learns to sew.

Instead, she makes lists. Of random thoughts, accidental implications, and little vexing things.

When she picks them up from their father for the first time at the end of the weekend, she cries. She tries not to let them see her tears, but he has cut their hair. Six, maybe seven inches.

On the car ride home, she can barely speak. So, she pushes a CD into the dashboard slot and plays their song. Loud.

*I would like to reach out my hand*
*I may see you, I may tell you to run (on my way, on*
*my way)*
*You know what they say about the young*

*Send me on my way (on my way)*
*Send me on my way (on my way)*
*Send me on my way (on my way)*
*Send me on my way (on my way)*
*Send me on my way (on my way)*
*Send me on my way (on my way)*
*Send me on my way (on my way)*

For the three of them, it becomes an anthem.

The youngest says, *Scream it, Mom. Scream it from up on the very top of your lungs.*

She grabs a Mason jar from the kitchen cabinet, tells them something about her childhood, longs for them to hear the happiness in her voice.

*We caught fireflies*, she says, *but we always freed them after a while.*

She punctures the lid of the jar with a small screwdriver she keeps in the drawer. *So they can breathe,* she says, as they watch her closely, wide-eyed.

They go outside onto the grass together, and she shows them how it's done. One hand kept flat, waiting, the other cupped and waving through the air, eventually a dome that will sit atop its foundation, a firefly's light spilling through each space between her fingers.

They both hesitate at first then begin to imitate her movements. Soon the jar has fifteen or twenty fireflies crawling up its glass walls.

Back inside, she switches off the light in the living room. Both girls slide off the couch cushions down onto the floor, closer to the jar on the coffee table.

Tiny lights flicker. Her daughters don't move; they hardly even blink.

Before bed, they go back outside, give the fireflies a chance to get away. Some of them disappear quickly. Others linger.

They wait. The oldest yawns a few times.

After she tucks them into bed, she sits alone in the living room for at least an hour, thinking about what it is she hasn't told her daughters. About her own childhood. Because it hurts too much for her to believe that she ever plucked the light organs from these beautiful creatures, that she ever smeared the bioluminescence on her face, like war paint.

It would shatter her if they were to know.

There are times, after she pays the rent, the utility bills, and the daycare, when she has to choose between buying bread and milk or using those dollars to do the laundry.

She learns fast how to live with less.

Learns to define happiness in other ways. To be content.

And she wants her daughters to know this, too. To appreciate the value of simplicity. Of just being.

It takes months for her to read *Little Women* to them. And there are plenty of times she wants to give up. Because they are not interested. They are distracted.

They are mad at her when she insists.

But she keeps reading. She wants to give them a chance to love the characters as much as she did when she was a young girl.

Or maybe she wants them to question the unfair limits put on girls and women back then, to see in this story what she'd failed to see for so long.

She tells them about the *Little Women* dolls she had when she was a young girl.

How, in her bedroom, the dolls in their fancy dresses were to be kept on shelves. On display. Her mother had said to her, over and over: *They are to look at, not touch.*

But, whenever she knew her mother wasn't close by, she'd take the dolls down from the shelves, play with them. Sometimes she'd change their story. More often, she quoted the book directly: *I can't get over my disappointment in being a girl,* the Jo March doll would always say.

She keeps a detailed ledger of loss:

one

In the middle of the night, the oldest screams, wakes her.

In the bathroom, three large bugs scurry across the floor.

With a shoe, she smacks hard at them. Like the crack of a bullet, each time, her daughter shudders.

She cringes at the damage. The crunch and scatter of exoskeleton and limbs.

One gets away.

Her daughter looks up. Consoles her. This goes on, becomes a nightly ritual.

She wants her daughters to know what it looks like to be unafraid.

Together, the three of them learn: Cockroaches can be as big as two inches long. And they can live for weeks without their heads.

two


They take flight, land again. Make themselves
another home.

The butterfly lady brings them milkweed, the tiniest
eggs. Together, they learn about life cycles and
letting go.

For her, a math of forgiveness. For each life taken,
one freed.

She confesses to her daughters: *I once pinned these
beautiful creatures to boards.*

*I am sorry.*

The youngest pats her on the back. The oldest
assures her it'll be okay. It is impossible for them to
understand the magnitude of her regret.

They construct their own wings out of tissue paper,
pipe cleaners, string. Pretend they can fly.

*Be careful,* she wants to say. But, instead, she flaps
her arms out to the side, whispers: *Just think about
far away.*

three


For a while, almost every morning around two o'clock, screams wake her.

The youngest punches at nothing but air. At the clowns of night-circuses. At monsters risen from her father's dark canvases, his rage-at-having-been-left come to life.

His absence howls in these quietest hours, bores itself through his daughter's tiny heart.

Nights are long. She wraps her arms around her daughter's body, holds on. She considers how much of motherhood is spent in silence, waiting, searching for ways to console.

To write some other story.

Without monsters and clowns.

With a father who attends school concerts and summer camp shows. Who doesn't take a pair of dull scissors to his daughters' beautiful hair.

four, five, six


When her grandmother's dying shifts from slowly to suddenly, she has no time to think, to react, to sweep her youngest daughter out of the room into the hallway of the nursing home.

No time to protect her from seeing the rattle of her grandmother's chest, then its stillness. From hearing the gasps, then the silence.

From knowing the time of death.

Then its permanence.

❦

In the midst of the divorce, she takes them to her parents' house. Sometimes, out of necessity, to check on them. Other times, it is the perfect distraction for her daughters, a constant in the midst of uncertainty.

In the side yard, a massive oak, a system of large roots ascending, breaking through the soil, looking for air. On the biggest ones, her daughters try to balance, arms out to the side, one foot carefully in front of the other.

Their willowy limbs tremble, wobble and flutter. When they slip off, it seems as though they are falling from a balance beam or a tightrope, a place much higher than inches from the ground.

So much depends on perception.

On the lowest branch of the oak, she ties the thick rope of a tire swing, loops and knots it several times. Her oldest daughter goes first. The limb bends slightly as the swing arcs higher and higher. The leaves rustle in rhythmic movement. Her daughters call them *tree-hands,* smiling and laughing at how it seems like they're waving to them.

The youngest searches the ground for the one leaf that mirrors best the shape of her own hand.

Small. Five lobes.

After trying several out, holding each one up against her palm, she finally finds the perfect leaf.

Proud, she presses it hard against her hand, bends her fingers into the notches between the lobes, and says, *Look, Mommy! I'm holding hands with the tree.*

❧

Too often, she dashes through life, forgetting to live it along the way, as though unpunctuated.

As though refusing to heed signs, despite their bright orange and yellow and red. Stop. Yield. Do Not Enter. Detour. Dead End.

Not pausing to take note of the spaces trying to insert themselves in between. In between one massive stroke then another. A father left paralyzed on the left side. In between each fall when he starts trying to walk again with a cane.

Her daughters stand somewhere close by, make themselves invisible, watch as she learns to somehow hoist his body back onto the chair or the bed.

In each room of her parents' house, the silence insists on being heard.

Caesura.

She tries to catch her breath.

But the music starts playing. Again. Each time, one less chair.

She stops attempting to sit down at all.

It is her mother next, not far behind. Pneumonia. COPD. A cannula and plastic tubing tether her to the hiss and click of an oxygen machine. It is hard to see. To hear. All of it.

The music stops. Again. And she wants to collapse onto the floor. Cry. Be comforted.

Her daughter turns to her and asks, *How come Nana keeps running out of air?*

❧

In the fickle-weather time between fall and winter, she keeps finding dead things.

She is of three minds.

In her thirteenth way of looking at a blackbird, she notices small pieces of grit in the gut, the neck snapped, head resting on the splayed feathers of its warped accordion wing.

Right away, she shields her daughters from seeing it, but knows she'll want to capture its decay.

Time-lapse. Maxilla hinged open. The v-shaped breach of its beak.

At night, she tries to sing her daughters lullabies. But the words catch, lodge like small bones in her throat. Stay there. Strangled love songs.

In the silence, thoughts come to her syntactically. Most often, two base forms adding themselves together. *Elsewhere. Foreshadow. Windpipe. Moonlight. Wishbone. Blackbird.*

*Heartbreak.*

---

*I was of three minds,* Wallace Stevens begins his poem, "Thirteen Ways of Looking at a Blackbird," a title some say alludes to the Cubist practice of incorporating into unity and stasis a number of possible views of the subject observed over a span of time.

Too much compounding. Adding up.

She chronicles the ruin of every little thing, holds her
daughters close. On weekends, she writes pantoums,
an a-b-a-b rhyme scheme linked by repeated lines, in
which, over and over again, she perhapses some other
life.

# math lessons

Not long after the divorce is final, she takes her daughters camping. Joins friends for a weekend in Promised Land State Park.

The only single mom, she wears her Scarlet S, tries not to let the uncertainty and doubt slip in.

*Did I do the right thing?* She keeps asking herself, *taking these two little girls away from their father, dividing everything in half, taking away any chance they might've had to think love is an infinite number.*

Her thoughts now sometimes veer off like this. Jumbled. Complex. No order of operations, nothing held safe inside brackets or parentheses, solved there first.

But she knows she needs to do this, to take them places, to make these kinds of memories. For her daughters. For herself. For the three of them.

Everyone prepares to go down to the lake: backpacks slung over shoulders, kayaks and canoes hoisted high above heads. They join the parade, one daughter on either side of her. Two hands. Two girls. Simple math. No remainder.

On the rocks along the edge of the lake, her daughters begin collecting sticks, piling them up—*walls*, they say, when asked, *to protect us in case the lake gets bigger and bigger.*

She wonders what makes them think of this—the need to fortify, to contain, to hold back what might threaten to harm. *What fantasies have prompted these elaborate stick piles, this make-pretend peril?*

Four minus one.

*By taking them away, had I opened up a place for fear to lodge itself?*

No one ever wants to say, *I am fragile.*

Someone offers her a canoe, suggests she take her daughters out onto the lake.

And she does.

She buckles them into life vests, climbs into the boat first and reaches out as a friend lifts them one at a time into her arms. She can feel her heart pumping harder and faster as they are pushed off shore with a kind of force that rocks the canoe back and forth. She almost drops the oars, convinced they are going to capsize.

One of the girls asks if they are going to tip over.

*No, I got this,* she says, trying to sound confident. She tightens her grip on the oars, begins to slowly row them out toward the middle of the lake.

Sometimes, the oars smack up against something underwater. She looks carefully over the side of the boat, sees tree stumps not too far beneath the surface. More of them than she thinks she'll see out in the middle of a lake. Though even one would have been more than she'd expect.

It is odd to think trees once stood here. Odder to consider the idea that someone once suggested they be chopped down in order to flood the area and make a lake.

For some reason, she thinks of the game Rock, Paper, Scissors, and how Water would beat them all if it were to ever be included.

For about fifteen to twenty minutes, the boat is steady. She is calmer. But doubt catches up with her again as she looks at their faces peeking out over the top of orange life jackets that have nearly obscured their entire bodies.

Two of them.

One of her.

This is where the math becomes an impossible word problem: *If a boat tips over and there is only one parent...*

She paddles them back to shore.

On the blackboard, she writes at least a hundred times:

It is notable to have tried; such ambition can never be wrong.

On days when her daughters are sick, she hides them away, secrets hushed beneath her drawing table in the department of Marketing Services.

Paper and a bin of magic markers all she has to keep them busy.

The oldest holds up the blue of sky. *What makes these markers magic?* she whispers.

*You do,* her mother says. *Look at those magical places you've brought to life. The sun and the moon and the stars all inhabiting the same sky. See the kind of light that kindles. And your birds. Look how you've given them bright feathered wings to fly.* She smiles at her daughter, asks how she's feeling.

*Better,* she says. *I'm making a beautiful place for you.* She folds herself, tucks her legs under her body, to fit better in the too-small space beneath the table.

Her time as a mother feels hurried. Too often divided and divided again and divided again: Work. Graduate school. Caretaking (or is it caregiving?)—one parent, two paralyzing strokes, the other, chronic lung disease.

She looks for ways to slow it down. To stay in the moment with her young daughters. To remember that this will be their story. These moments filled with light and color, shape and contour, will someday be distilled down to impression.

Proof.

It will be what they mimic, how they might pattern their own lives someday.

In fall, they collect leaves, arrange them beneath sheets of paper.

They peel the labels from crayons, lay them down, slide them across the blank page. In each streak of Sunglow, Copper, Goldenrod, the pattern of a leaf emerges.

The oldest notes the symmetry, the matching network of veins on either side of the stem.

Semblance.

They both look closely at her hands, trace, with their small fingers, the raised pattern of blue veins branching and crisscrossing. They ask why they are blue. She explains how arteries carry oxygenated blood away from the heart and veins carry oxygen-poor blood back from the body to the heart.

How this pumping back and forth is the only way they can stay alive.

The youngest asks if her heart is going to stop pumping someday. If she's going to die, like her grandmother.

# reading lessons

*Books are living beings,* she tells her daughters, *look how they line up like that in their dust jackets with their tall straight spines. Sometimes, when it's quiet, I can hear them breathing.*

She wants them to be amazed.

The oldest, when she's alone in her room, imitates how her mother reads to her each night. She lines up Pooh and Piglet, Eeyore and Tigger, gets them ready for Story Time.

In this Preparatory School for Aspiring Mothers, she turns the first few pages and begins: *Ponce-uh-wonna-time...*

When fall comes around one year, her youngest daughter collects the brightest reds and yellows the season has to offer, fills the pockets of her sweatshirt and jacket with as many leaves as she can.

Her eyes widen with excitement as she searches, more and more, with each treasure she stows away.

Days later, when she shoves her hands into those same pockets, she pulls out fists full of brown flakes. Crumbled and dry. As she watches the tiny pieces cascade to the floor, disappointment tugs at the corners of her mouth, fills her eyes with tears.

*It is never easy*, she thinks, *knowing I can't preserve the wide-eyed wonder of my child.*

Somewhere, she reads: "The veins that move water into a leaf are choked off once it is severed from the branch, at a place called the abscission layer."

Abscission is a process, she learns. It occurs during resorption, when leaves are changing colors. It occurs during the formation of a protective layer of cells or stroma. It occurs during detachment, a breaking apart or shedding.

It feels like the space between mother and child, magnifying microscopically each day.

*I am doing everything I can,* she wants to say to her daughters. *Sometimes, it is impossible to understand. To reconcile the fragility of this world.*

She tires finally, from years of doing this alone.

Swallows and nuthatches make of her body a home, perch on her splintered limbs, stilled for moments only, never long enough to mend.

Sometimes, she imagines letting them assemble nests in the chestnut strands of her hair. And, with her daughters beside her, she offers each bird a verse from the book they read at bedtime: poems by Edna St. Vincent Millay:

> *My candle burns at both ends; it will not last the night; but ah, my foes, and oh, my friends—it gives a lovely light.*

⚜

On weekends, sometimes, in the middle of their new apartment, she sets up an art table. Her daughters carry kitchen chairs across the living room and the three of them sit for hours making pictures.

They draw animals and flowers and trees.

They draw their new "house," a row of brick apartments, theirs with a big letter O on the outside door.

After dinner, she has an idea, suggests they trace their hands over and over, fill in each one with different shades of green. Crayon. Colored pencil. Tempera paint. Watercolor.

She doesn't tell her daughters what she plans to do with them. Just says she needs a lot.

> pine, fern, moss, chartreuse, emerald, olive, seafoam, pear, sage, juniper, asparagus, jade, bottle, bright, forest, jungle, Granny Smith, grass, iguana, meadow, pale, spring, spruce

They work until bedtime, quiet mostly. Focused. In these moments, she feels peace again. Feels like she made the right choice, taking them away from a father who had been taking that peace away from them.

After she tucks them into bed, she sits for hours alone cutting out thirty or forty of their green hands. From one of the empty moving boxes, she traces and cuts out a cardboard ring. All around this circle, she pastes their big and small hands. Overlaps them. Interweaves their fingers. Until it all begins to look like the greenery on a wreath.

On the front door, a nail already there, she hangs what she's made, excited to show her daughters in the morning.

So much has changed for them. She wants—needs—to create a place filled with things that are familiar. Things that become constant. Certain. A compass for them, pointing, reassuring: *This is home. This is home.*

In the crowded corridor of the School for Unwound Mothers, seconds before the bell rings, she drops everything she's trying to balance—a precarious pile of books and lunchboxes, Beanie Babies and My Little Ponies.

(On a good day, she laughs.
On a bad day, she drinks
vodka like it's lemonade.)

She wants to be confident, unflinching, but uncertainty occupies even the smallest of spaces in between.

She keeps repeating what becomes her quiet refrain:

*No coward soul is mine.*

*No coward soul is mine.*

*No coward soul is mine.*

*No coward soul is mine.*

*No coward soul is mine.*

*No coward soul is mine.*

*No coward soul is mine.*

For Emily Brontë, it had been both title and first line.

❦

Bartram's Covered Bridge over Crum Creek becomes their favorite place. Saturday picnics.

Hours spent practicing crossing the creek on the biggest rocks. She holds their hands, one at a time. Always, the other left behind.

This careful navigation.

On her way across, the oldest talks about how the water moves, how it goes around the rocks, ripples and makes a gurgling sound. The youngest notices how fast leaves and sticks are moved along. How sunlight hits the surface, makes it look like glass.

She can only concentrate.

Sometimes, being a mother is an act of contrition.

She wants to be in the moment with them, to celebrate their innocence and wonder, but she can't. Her body is the hum of breath held, bones calibrated. Worry drains her, the constant burden of thinking her daughters might slip and fall.

In the condo they move into next, they finally have a place to hang their coats. Something about that gesture feels like hope to her.

Like home.

Her youngest daughter sits on the floor and sorts through the winter hats and scarves inside the big wicker basket where they're stored. In the hallway, she takes all of the gloves and mittens she's found and lines them up, side by side. *There are so many mittens that don't have a match,* she says. *I wonder where the other ones go.*

In the Cloakroom of Proper Musings and Far Too Many Unmatched Mittens, she slips a right-handed royal blue mitten onto one hand, a right-handed chartreuse mitten onto the other.

And, as if they're sock puppets, she presses them together in a kiss, declares them a pair.

In another lifetime, she studied typography, letters in need of kerning, tracking, ample room to turn themselves into words. And leading, too, always the possibility of more space between the lines.

Before she became a mother, she spent some of her days floating aimlessly in the counter of **O**, curling up with a good book along the loop of **P**, sleeping late within the eye of lowercase **e.**

Now she finds herself dangling from the finial of a double-storey **a**, tippy-toes reaching for the arm of **T**, tripping sometimes over the serif-feet of capital **I.**

Too often, she feels alone, even when she's surrounded by language, that legion of ascenders and descenders she's lined up, in some attempt to make sense of it all.

# art lessons

She looks out the window, tells her daughters how the trees in winter, bare and brown, make her feel sad sometimes.

She wants to curl her body into the s of sleep. Stay dormant until spring arrives.

Her daughters, as they often do, try to make her happy again.

The two of them sit at the art table in the middle of the room, decide they want to draw the winter trees. The youngest motions for her to sit, hands her the Fuzzy Wuzzy brown crayon.

As they begin, they both remind her how much easier drawing a tree might be when they don't need to worry about the leaves.

She pauses, lets their words sink in. She'd never considered it that way, never thought to *worry* about drawing leaves.

As they make line drawings—curves and arches, curls and squiggles—she can see their struggle, their hesitation to let go of whatever control they have over the marks they're making. They want to be precise. Perfect.

She talks about how the process of making art should be fun. How they should let go of their worry.

They both stop for a moment, look up, say they want to tell her a secret.

They lower their voices, almost to a whisper. The oldest says: *Dad makes us draw in pencil first. And erase a lot. Erase our mistakes.* The youngest adds: *And sometimes he fixes what we draw so it looks right.*

She presses down on her crayon so hard it snaps in half.

She wants to tell them not to listen to their father, that he's a perfectionist and he is ruining art for them. That he'll ruin everything if they let him.

Instead, she smiles, thanks them for making winter trees with her, rummages through a drawer for magnets so she can hang them on the refrigerator when they've finished.

As Captain of the Synchronized Swimming Team, she knows something about treading water, something about depth.

No one ever warns her: The world is a shallow place.

She needs to offer her daughters new meaning for the word *reflection*. A chance to see themselves in another light.

She shows them her scars, traces each line with the tip of her finger. *It took months after the car accident before I could glimpse my own face.*

*Back then, everyone kept saying pretty to me, until it sounded like a promise.*

For days, weeks, she can see only the ceiling tiles in her fluorescent room. Shadows shifting, light to dark, the measure of each day.

She can hear only the beep and click of machines, tethered. The tick of a clock on the wall. Time to think. To dig deeper.

*A kind of excavation*, she tells her daughters. *My body already cracked wide open. Rib cage. Mandible. Spine.*

*Inside, I found words, started arranging them on the page.*

She is desperate to save her girls.

# swimming lessons

The summer her oldest daughter turns seven, she wants to jump from the diving board into the deep end of a pool. She begs. Her mother agrees, but only if she is there to catch her.

She bounces for a while on the end of the board, her knobby knees bent slightly, her lips turning a light shade of violet.

Then, all of a sudden, her body is in midair, a blur of blue bathing suit, limbs, splashing as she breaks the water's surface.

But she doesn't jump out far enough.

In a single moment, she drops to the bottom of the pool.

Nine feet down.

Numbers lurch through her mind. Whole numbers. Fractions. Depths. Percentages. Odds.

Her daughter had only been able to hold her breath to the count of sixteen-Mississippi when they'd practiced earlier in the shallow end.

She dives straight down, adrenaline pumping her heart so fast she is dizzy.

*Thirteen-Mississippi. Fourteen-Mississippi.*

Her daughter kicks.

*Fifteen-Mississippi.*

Flails her arms.

*Sixteen-Mississippi.*

Finally, she slips beneath her daughter's slender body, propels her upward until she finds air. Coughs and gurgles. But her mother remains underwater. No strength left in her arms. No air left in her lungs.

If she gives up, they will both sink back down.

*Not now*, she thinks. *Not. Now.*

Moments of panic weave themselves into a network of nerve fibers.

Tangle.

Stay.

Her body remembers.

# baking lessons

Midday, she wakes, her fever breaking.

She has no idea how much time has passed. No idea what her daughters have been doing while she'd been sleeping.

She listens for them, worries at the silence, shuffles down hall.

They giggle as she turns the corner, each of them holding onto the same plate. The Easy-Bake-Oven cake on it is lopsided, covered in patchy peaks of bright pink icing.

In their squeaky voices, they sing *Happy Birthday* to her.

She doesn't notice the carpet until she walks toward the kitchen. Stops, stares down in disbelief.

*We're sorry, Mommy. We didn't mean to do that*, the oldest says.

*It was an accident*, the youngest mumbles into a blankie she holds up to her mouth.

*We tried to clean it up.*

They had only rubbed it in, made it worse. Pink food coloring, tan rug. She feels the urge to yell, to be angry with both of them. But she holds back, tears coming instead.

She cries because she feels sick. And alone. She cries because her daughters have tried so hard to make her happy. She cries because she has made so many decisions that have changed their lives. Forever.

*We didn't mean to make you cry.*

She hugs them both, pulls them in close to her, buries her face in the hair their father has scissored to shoulder-length.

Her head pounds. Her throat feels raw. But she knows she'll want to remember this moment. Long after the pink stain fades away. Long after they leave this place.

There will be other birthdays. Many she won't remember. A number changing. Again. And again. There will be cards her daughters will make for her and small gifts they'll sculpt or glue or paint.

But it is that lopsided pink cake she'll never forget.

*Some things break us open,* she thinks.

*Quietly.*

*Slowly.*

*And we are never the same.*

✣

In the Principal's Office, she types up notes.
Permission notes. Gold-starred notes commending
herself for trying hard.

Excuse notes.

Please excuse _ _ _ _ _ _ _ _ _ _ _ _ _ _ _ _ _ _ _ _ _ _ _
for being absent / late / tired / uninvolved /
stressed / sad / angry ...

Please check the reason(s) below:

_ _ _ _ _ Illness

_ _ _ _ _ Death of a family member

_ _ _ _ _ Court appearance

_ _ _ _ _ Fulltime job

_ _ _ _ _ Freelance job

_ _ _ _ _ Deadbeat father

_ _ _ _ _ Overdrawn bank account

_ _ _ _ _ Other (please explain)

❧

In a house they move to next, tall and made of stone, her daughter builds a birdhouse in the backyard. When it weathers to warped, when only three walls remain, she knows.

It is time for them to go.

Again.

They are migratory.

She plans their departure.

Makes lists: cardboard boxes, packing tape.

> Leave: the tiny bones of goldfish in the garden.

> Take: the statue of Buddha, the floribunda rose tree.

Somewhere, inside a wall, beneath a floorboard, behind a radiator cover, she thinks of hiding small things that made up a life here, their story: Half-burned birthday candles. A broken robin's egg. A ball of unwound string.

There are secrets a house knows. She tries to hush them, sweep them over thresholds out into the night. Some, like shadows, have lurched into corners, petaled out from the foyer, the kitchen, the attic, to places unseen.

She wants someone to walk through the rooms with her, up the stairs. To tell her how long before the tangle of hair leaves the drain, before their fingerprints are wiped from the windows, before the three-walled birdhouse is taken by the wind.

# bike riding lessons

After trying so many times she loses count, she finally resorts to hiring the young woman who works at the bicycle shop where she buys the matching silver ten-speed Schwinns for her daughters.

The oldest is fine. She pedals along the sidewalk, disappears around the corner without looking back. The worry about her will be one of too much distance. Houses, streets, miles, adding up in between. How to keep her safe once freedom is discovered.

The youngest is more afraid. There had been a "bicycle incident" years before, one even training wheels could not prevent. A gravel path where she'd fall, tear open her elbows and knees, her chin and nose, tiny stones imbedding themselves beneath her skin.

So, years later, the ten-speed Schwinn will be too much. Still. She fears falling, even with the hot-pink helmet, the knee and elbow pads.

In their playhouse, her daughters take turns being the teacher.

She overhears them, smiles.

*Prepositions are relationship words,* the oldest says. *They can never be alone.*

On the day she gets remarried, her daughters both cling to her white and gold sequined dress. They hold on so tight it seems as if they believe she'll fly away if they happen to let go.

She wonders, as she says *I do,* what they must be thinking. Do they question what makes this any different than the last time, when she married their father?

Out on the dance floor at the reception, her daughters spin around her like tiny planets orbiting the sun.

The youngest, with owl-like eyes, fidgets, bites her nails. Ruffles her feathers. There is no way to comfort her, no words to reassure.

They move into a new house with the second husband, the stepfather.

It never feels like home to her.

It is too big. Too filled with noise.

There are six children now. Two *steps* for him. Four *steps* for her. She wants to call it a *blended* family, but that would be far too buoyant a word.

She tries to find peace where she can.

Then a family of squirrels finds its way in, scratches and squeals inside the walls.

In the lunchroom of the Finishing School for Mothers Who Never Really Considered Themselves Suitable for Domestic Life, she tries to pry the spoon from another day-old bowl of dried-up Kraft Easy Mac & Cheese.

# vocabulary lessons

She discovers hundreds of synonyms for *grief,* writes them all down.

Gives a few of them a story of their own.

## regret:

For months, she reads "The Walrus and the Carpenter" to them at bedtime. She has memorized every stanza, likes the cadence, the alternate end-rhyme.

When she finishes reading one night, her oldest daughter says, *That's not nice, Mommy. Why do they eat the oysters like that?*

Once her daughters are both asleep, she returns to the poem, goes back over each line.

"A loaf of bread," the Walrus said, / "Is what we chiefly need: / Pepper and vinegar besides / Are very good indeed-- / Now if you're ready, Oysters dear, / We can begin to feed."

She wonders, sitting alone in the back of the room at the Summer School for Failing Mothers: *How did I not notice what was happening all along?*

&

## misery:

She is not quite forty when they take from her body the nest where she nurtured her babies, where she kept them safe and warm.

Afterwards, in a haze of morphine, she is sent back to the School of New Mothers, banished to a dark room at the end of the hall.

There are still bullies here, but this time they make her listen to the cries of newborns, see them pass by her door, a parade of fertile mothers, still aglow with life-giving, slowly pushing their tiny ones along in pink-and-blue-ribboned islets.

Her abdomen aches. Her cheeks flush.

She leans over the bedrail, throws up on the floor.

&

## dismay:

Her youngest daughter comes to her for help with a school project. She needs to devise a way to drop a raw egg without breaking it.

Her daughter has ideas.

As a mother, she has doubt, mostly, a nagging feeling that this experiment will only end up disappointing her.

She listens as her daughter speaks fast, details the boundless potential of her ideas, and wonders what makes her so confident she can somehow protect something as fragile as an egg.

But her mother doesn't want to be the one to discourage her, so she stays quiet.

And they begin.

Her first idea. Materials: packing tape, bubble wrap.

Other than helping her to secure these two materials, she wants to do the rest on her own. She focuses, her hands in constant motion, folding layers of padded plastic around the egg, tearing off pieces of tape and adhering them to an expanding cushioned orb.

When she finishes, they stand side by side at the open second floor window. She turns toward her mother, holds the protected egg at arm's length, just beyond the windowsill, lets it go.

By the time they stick their heads out the window to watch it fall, it has already landed down below.

On the driveway, her daughter kneels on the asphalt, carefully peels back the layers of tape and bubble wrap, stops when she sees the yellowish liquid of the egg.

*Perhaps she'd wrapped the egg too tightly and it had cracked before she'd even dropped it.*

*But how is a mother supposed to tell her child that it's possible to protect something too much?*

despair:

She tries to take them somewhere nice. A room with a view, a balcony on the third floor.

There is no way she can predict what's coming. What will arrive soon.

First, a boy. Innocent enough, at first. But, eventually, they will call him stalker-boy. And she'll have to ask security guards to help protect her daughters and their two friends.

How many times has she wanted to warn all the girls and women, keeping her own monster stories hidden away? Stories of shadow-men carrying knives. Of sad men and their wandering eyes. Of lying men, with Italian leather soles, betraying their wives.

By now, she should know better.

Next, a storm. Tropical, at first. But, eventually, they'll call it a hurricane.

Wind picks up the ocean, heaves it onto land. Together, from the balcony, they watch the battering of trees, water rising to fill rooms on the first floor.

Through the night, they hold on. Try to think about other things.

In the calm of morning, she wonders what has become of this storm. Did it weaken out at sea or pick up momentum along a path inland, intensify?

And she wonders, too, what becomes of stalker-boys? Do they end up turning into bigger monsters on the dark, lonely Island of Stalker-Men?

woe:

In their story, she reminds them, princes are imaginary.

And fairy godmothers fall hard from the sky, their wings clipped by sharp words and paring knives.

She needs her daughters to know: *Happily ever...* never comes before *...after.*

*Fairytales are the worst kind of fiction.*

Perhaps her warning comes too late, though. One boy's fist, balled in rage, already having struck the perfect bones of her oldest daughter's face.

Sometimes, she thinks, there is no way out, only hundreds of wrong ways through. Pages and pages of language in need of amending. Excising.

*This is a poem to protect you,* she says, before erasing every line.

She wants to go back, hide inside the forts they fashioned out of bed sheets, the simple pinch of a clothespin keeping out the beasts.

In the Library of Abundant Criticism and Unspeakable Blame, she accrues late fees for overdue books. She struggles to absolve herself, to give herself a break.

# driving lessons

After weeks, she finally resorts to hiring a professional driver's education teacher. There is no way for her to adequately brace herself in the front seat beside her sixteen-year-old daughter.

*Brake! Yellow light! Curb! Stop sign! Curve!*

She has spent far too many days in the Auditorium of Accidents and Aftermaths, knows intimately the force of impact, the ways a body can break.

How fear will come on stage, absolutely slay its audition, leave her spellbound, go on to play a leading role in *The Doomsayer Diaries, a Catastrophizing Show for Mothers of Sixteen-Year-Olds.*

She anticipates the future that awaits them, as they hurry away to the land of grown-ups.

It is hard for her not to say, *Sit awhile. Watch the magnolia tree bloom. Sip Darjeeling tea with me. Slow down.*

She learns fast: the teen years are one long board game, some strange unrelenting loop of Trouble, Battleship, Risk, Twister, Chutes and Ladders.

It is impossible to know which set of rules to play by on any given day.

And there are pop quizzes, too, almost every day. Never graded on a curve. No extra credit.

Sometimes, she sits at her desk and cries. Just when she thinks she knows everything, there is something else to learn.

She can hardly keep up.

When the "purple hair incident" takes place, she can't decide if it's a mishap or yet another challenging test in the Advanced Placement Psychology Class for Mothers of Teenage Girls.

# photography lessons

They can't go back.

But she tries, spends hours sifting through boxes of photographs.

It gets harder for her to breathe the more she realizes how few photos there are of her with her daughters. But she keeps sorting, her fingertips grazing the edge of moments, moving swiftly back and forth through time.

She finds one she'd taken of the two of them walking ahead of her on the beach in California, their blond and brown hair tangled together in the wind.

She is there, behind them. Composing the shot.

She finds one of her youngest daughter walking toward the security line at the airport on the day she moves to Germany.

She is there, too, behind her. Composing the shot.

Because, sometimes, as a mother, being outside the frame is the only way for her to stay connected. Every family needs a photographer.

And it helps her to hold on. To keep from forgetting. To keep busy so she doesn't cry.

She finds pictures of both daughters together in costumes on Halloween. On Christmas morning, opening presents in front of the tree. First-missing-tooth photos. First-day-of-school. Riding a bicycle. Driving a car. Moving into a dorm room.

Finally, she finds a few of the three of them. They are in Atlantic City. A day trip. She doesn't know what year it is, but they are both in college. She remembers asking several strangers to take the pictures, thinking at the time how few opportunities they had to be together like this.

Revel, the casino they are standing beside in one of the photographs, is gone now.

But she considers the name, the word and its meaning, anyway. She has always been drawn to definitions.

She likes this one best: *Unrestrained merrymaking.*

And this: *To engage in uproarious festivities. To bask in the self-reflected glow of your own pleasure.*

*If you revel in something, you're not just pleased or even excited; you're overwhelmed by joy.*

On the beach near a jetty in front of the casino, they pose again. She's in the middle, her arms around each of her daughters. All three of them are wearing sunglasses. Smiling. And, just seconds after the photo is taken, a wave breaks hard on the back of their legs, splashing and soaking them.

Outside the frame, for what seems like forever, they laugh until it hurts.

She brings along a shovel and a spade.

Each time, in the Schoolyard of Gray Granite Stones and Perpetual Grief, they tread through uncut grass, trampling it, forging their own path to her parents' grave.

Her daughters sit beside one another, dig up dandelions, liberate worms from soil they've been sharing with the dead.

Too often, there's another body to bury.

Summer here, bursting with life. Overbent willows and upright oaks. Sparrows, starlings, and jays. Tidy stem-cut bunches of flowers left as offerings—ribbon-tied daisies, floribunda roses in a beer-glass vase.

She looks around, reads aloud some of the etched names. *Neighbors,* she thinks. To the right of her parents. To the left.

At the base of their granite stone, she arranges bright orange marigolds in a perfect line, pushes the wooden stick of a pinwheel into the ground.

She teaches her daughters how to build altars. How to grieve.

In between, she teaches her daughters to find places among the living to plant trees.

In another country together for the first time, they learn here on the side of the road how to eat an apricot, how to twist and pry flesh from stone.

The three of them wander into churches in towns of bell towers and steeples, offer up prayers beside shrines to the beatified. She sees her daughters watching her, wondering what it means to pray. They lace their fingers together, half-close their eyes.

Elsewhere, the world is coming apart—there are people destroying the planet, preying on the weak— and she can no longer call to mind what it might mean to protect. To be protected.

On the last day of their trip, she tilts the wick of one candle to light another. Wax drips and she cries for the death of the woman she once was, before she lost her own mother, before she understood that she'd have to leave her own daughters someday.

She starts taking night classes at
The Academy of Trepidation, strives to
reach her full potential, double-majors
in Doubt and Misgivings.

She wonders what her daughters will recall of childhood once they leave the shelter of its dunes, paddle through the deepest water, struggle to find a way somehow to circumvent the Island of Unfit Fathers.

To go beyond.

They walk toward the edge of Coopers Rock, the three of them, talk about the idea of home, how it keeps shifting. Is shifting again now. About the miles and days multiplying in between.

Her oldest daughter has found this place. For hours, they've been winding along country roads.

Vast bands of rock cliffs line the river gorge. Below, the roar of water. They take a thousand pictures, sit beside one another, give themselves a little more time before goodbye.

She touches her hand to letters etched into boulders, wanting to carve their names, something to last beyond this moment, long after the Mountain Laurel bloom. Long after she turns to leave.

Together, they construct a language for being apart, borrowed words from a long history of mothers and daughters.

Her oldest daughter has made a life for herself here, learned fast to adapt, a map of the city's underground already stored inside her head.

*Meanwhile*, she keeps thinking. That word inserting itself, again and again, placeholder for all the time in between.

*Meanwhile.*

This shift in the patterns of their exchange.

She follows her daughter down stairs onto platforms beside tracks. Everything between them measured by the length of each stay. She practices the vocabulary of visitor, listens more, hastens her step, finds ways to fit in.

Here, now, far beyond wishing back, they both hang onto what is.

Fine-tune.

Edit.

Modify.

They avoid the rhetoric of politics, search for places to sip wine.

*Meanwhile.*

The youngest moves to Munich.

Motherhood nearly crushes her sometimes.

Had she forgotten years ago to mention what exactly she'd meant by *far away* or *beyond*? She wishes she'd been more specific to begin with, or perhaps later written a lengthy dissent on the idea of *transatlantic*.

The meaning of the word consumes her, language always layering up like it does.

> *: negotiating : traversing : navigating : going over*

> *: crossing or being beyond the Atlantic Ocean*

> *: located on or coming from the other side of the Atlantic Ocean*

> *: involving people or countries on both sides of the Atlantic Ocean*

*Atlantic Ocean: North Atlantic. South Atlantic. Atlantic Basin. 41,100,000 square miles, covering more than 20 percent of the Earth's surface with an average depth of 12,881 feet or 2,147 fathoms*

> *Fathom:* NOUN. *A unit of length equal to 6 feet used especially for measuring the depth of water*
>
> *Fathom:* VERB. *To understand the reason for something*

This new kind of long-distance mothering.

She can't possibly see any of it coming: The sobbing at songs on the radio. At reruns of *Dawson's Creek*. At empty cupcake tins stacked in the cupboard.

She tries not to talk about the distance in between. Or the six-hour time difference. Or the months that will go by.

It is too hard to fathom.

She searches for brilliant words, instead, the kind that will turn their moments together into shiny, lasting memories she feels desperate now to make.

Along the river, she picks up a stone the size of her fist. It is shaped like a heart—not the flat cartoon-kind, though. A three-dimensional, anatomical heart, water having smoothed its surface, tunneled its way through ventricles and atria, a single notched valve.

Her own heart has grown heavy.

She feels it, sits down beside her youngest daughter on the fallen trunk of a tree. Together, they watch two fish turn fast in the water, try to swim upstream.

*What can I tell her about the world*, she wonders, *that won't make us both want to cry?*

She lets herself take in what she knows to be true: two cities, two countries. Two continents plotted on a map. In between, an ocean, the arc of a curve four thousand miles long.

In this stitch of separation, she tries to hold on. To knot the thread over and over at its end, to keep herself from loosening, coming apart.

There are other stones she gathers, too, slipping them into pockets, planning to take them home with her. A suitcase weighed down by river rock.

And her sadness in leaving here is the kind that scoops up bird feathers they see together on a path. The kind that plucks petals from a red geranium in the plant box on her daughter's balcony. The kind that snaps photographs of sidewalk cafes where they've eaten ice cream or almost finished a stein of German beer.

If only to have something to hold onto. To remind.

Something that looks like protection. To reassure. She tries to memorize subway maps and airport signs, names of places she can hardly pronounce.

*There exists a kind of sadness that's like magic,* she thinks, looking out the airplane window. *Now you see it. Now you don't.*

*No one tells you about this trick.*

In the beginning, she thinks she'll be the kind of mother who will remember what her daughters' first words were. Or exactly how old they were when they took their first steps. Or lost their first tooth.

And, maybe, somewhere, she does write it all down. In a baby book someone gives her, knowing she might forget.

In the Graduate School of Older/Wiser Mothers, she finally offers herself forgiveness.

Finally, she gets an office. Small, like a confessional box.

She keeps it stocked with chocolate cake, butterscotch pie, bottles of Chardonnay.

# Acknowledgments

Several of these pieces first appeared, in slightly different form, in *Cobalt Review*, *december*, *Literary Mama*, *ep;phany*, *Blue Heron Review* and in my poetry chapbook, *No Such Place* (published by Finishing Line Press, 2013).

With appreciation for time spent writing over coffee with Autumn Konopka. And my gratitude to Christopher Eckman for his close reading and copy editing, his brilliant creative advice, and his loving friendship.

Thank you to the amazing people at Atmosphere Press, especially Nick Courtright, Lisa Mottolo, and Cameron Finch. And to Dover Publications for permission to use the illustrations in this book, from their *Pictorial Archive from Nineteenth-Century Sources (Women)*.

And to Anna Keiser for her talent in painting the cover background for this book.

# About Atmosphere Press

Atmosphere Press is an independent, full-service publisher for excellent books in all genres and for all audiences. Learn more about what we do at atmospherepress.com.

We encourage you to check out some of Atmosphere's latest releases, which are available at Amazon.com and via order from your local bookstore:

*Report from the Sea of Moisture,* poetry by Stuart Jay Silverman
*Eyeless Mind,* nonfiction by Stephanie Duesing
*Saint Lazarus Day,* short stories by R. Conrad Speer
*My Father's Eyes,* a novel by Michael Osborne
*The Lower Canyons,* a novel by John Manuel
*A Blameless Walk,* nonfiction by Charles Hopkins
*The Horror of 1888,* nonfiction by Betty Plombon
*Shiftless,* a novel by Anthony C. Murphy
*White Snake Diary,* nonfiction by Jane P. Perry
*From Rags to Rags,* essays by Ellie Guzman
*Connie Undone,* a novel by Kristine Brown
*The Enemy of Everything,* poetry by Michael Jones
*A Cage Called Freedom,* a novel by Paul P.S. Berg
*Giving Up the Ghost,* essays by Tina Cabrera
*Family Legends, Family Lies,* nonfiction by Wendy Hoke
*Shining in Infinity,* a novel by Charles McIntyre
*Buildings Without Murders,* a novel by Dan Gutstein
*The Stargazers,* poetry by James McKee
*SEED: A Jack and Lake Creek Book,* a novel by Chris S. McGee
*The Pretend Life,* poetry by Michelle Brooks
*Minnesota and Other Poems,* poetry by Daniel N. Nelson
*Southern. Gay. Teacher.,* nonfiction by Randy Fair

# About the Author

Kristina Moriconi is an essayist, poet, and visual artist whose work has appeared in a variety of literary journals and magazines. Her work has also been selected as a finalist in terrain.org's 2017 Nonfiction Contest, *december*'s 2018 & 2019 Curt Johnson Prose Award in Nonfiction, and awarded Honorable Mention in *Juncture*'s 2018 Memoir Contest. Moriconi currently teaches Creative Nonfiction in an MFA program in Pennsylvania. She is excited to be moving to Pittsburgh with her husband and two dogs.